NATURAL AFFINITIES

NATURAL AFFINITIES

POEMS

DAVID HECKER

MoonPathPress

Poetry
ISBN 978-1-936657-25-4

Cover art: *Madrona* by Sydni Sterling, acrylic on canvas.

Author photo: by Helen Hecker

Design by: Tonya Namura,
using Liberation Serif (text) and Arial Black (display).

MoonPath Press is dedicated to publishing the finest poets of
the U.S. Pacific Northwest.

MoonPath Press
PO Box 445
Tillamook, OR 97141

MoonPathPress@gmail.com

http://MoonPathPress.com

This book is dedicated to

Jeffrey & Michelle
and
Michelle & Shannon

ACKNOWLEDGMENTS

My gratitude to the editors and publishers of the following press and journals where these poems appeared, often in earlier versions.

Ars Poetica: "Horse Chestnut."

Crab Walk Press: "Desert," "Andalusia," "Sanctuary," "Departure," and "Immigrant."

Cirque Journal: "A Lucky Crab."

APPRECIATIONS

The writing of this collection of poems and many other poems began about fifteen years ago. I had advice, assistance, and criticism from many groups and individuals along the way, but I want especially to thank Lana Hechtman Ayers, editor and publisher of MoonPath Press, for her careful selection and arrangement of the poems in this volume. She also edited poems into more precise visions of the writer's intentions.

Early in the process of becoming a poet, I read a book by Dorianne Laux & Kim Addonizio, *The Poet's Companion: A Guide to the Pleasures of Writing Poetry.* Their suggestions for selecting topics for poems and exercises to follow resulted in some of the poems contained in this book. Other helpful books about poetry that I read included those by Mary Oliver, Charles Olson, Alfred Corn, Robert Wallace, Betsy Lerner, Louise Glück, Jane Hirshfield, Judson Jerome, Denise Levertov, Theodore Roethke, and William Stafford.

Reading many poets over the years in English and in translation increased my appreciation for the substance, artistry, and importance of this writing genre. I will not name them for the list is extensive, but I have put together a list of my favorite one hundred poems by the best poets for me.

Centrum Writer's Conferences, Hugo House presentations and classes also were important, but the Strawberry Hill writing group on Bainbridge Island led by John Willson and poet participants, including David Stallings, Kris Hotchkiss, Neil Doherty, Gary Anderson, Marit Saltrones, and Marlys Burnett over a period of several years, gave me the advice and suggestions that carried me over down periods and through many rewrites to finished poems, some of which are also part of this collection.

I'm grateful also for the opportunity to read poems at various locations, including Open Books, Frye Art Museum, Hugo House, Northwind Art Center, Poulsbohemian Coffeehouse, San Carlos Restaurant, and the Eagle Harbor Book Company.

Finally but not least of all, I thank my Helen and family for their constant encouragement.

CONTENTS

NATURAL AFFINITIES

I DEPARTURES

NEAR WHITE SHIELD (1962)

I'm alone and carry a rifle. Below zero and calm, the grasslands are covered with four inches of snow and deeper drifts with brush just sticking above a skin of shiny ice. The sky is gray with darkening clouds even though it is midday. I come across fresh tracks and follow them, cradling the rifle on one arm. As I step around a mound that resembles in size a large Mandan Indian winter lodge, I pause, sensing that a fox is circling to retreat in our combined footprints. Retracing my steps carefully to reduce the crunching sound until I reach the top of the circle, I crouch in the knee-high bushes, watching where the fox might appear. I hear mice scratching below the thin shield of frozen snow and recall an image from a National Geographic television program. In it a fox rears on its hind legs and drives its front quarters down into the snow, stiff-legged, hoping to crash through the surface and trap a mouse between its paws and the frozen ground below.

A red fox ambles into my view twenty feet away, until it sees me and stops, eyes widening and ears pricked. The sight of the red fox, with its sparkling eyes and shiny black whiskers, astonishes and reassures me, for he had attempted to evade but became an audience, reading my motives as another lonely hunter. I don't move or raise my rifle, a prop carried to justify solitude on this prairie land. This moment of recognition ends when the fox casually breaks eye contact and lopes off into the brush.

LEARNING IN NORTH DAKOTA

The gearshift rocks in my hand
as the Model A Ford lurches
down a gravel road.
At 14, chauffeur and surrogate son,
I ride high on a cushion.

Living with my grandma
and bachelor uncle, a carpenter,
I learn by day to pour concrete, shingle roofs,
strive by night to fathom girls.

"Stay clear of the shoulder,"
Uncle Charlie says, as I shift into high.
Hearing the differential gear grind,
I peer along the headlight beams
as if all this comes easy.

At a pyramid ridge left by a road grader,
I navigate into its edge,
react to the pull of the tire
by gripping the steering wheel
as if it might fly off.

Uncle Charlie says, "Keep it under forty,"
sings off-key
about being so lonesome
he might die,
about a bad conscience.

I ask what his song means.
He gives a half-smile,
sings again that favored line.

Stones smack our windshield
as other cars flicker by.
Slough crickets counter
Uncle Charlie's crooning.

A FADING RITUAL

I park my dad's old Buick, and my date
and I enter the cathedral-like church,
dip our fingers in holy water,
make the sign of the cross.

Facing us are silent aisles, vacant pews,
large columns, vaulted ceilings,
arches filled with stained glass windows,
a marble statue of the Virgin Mary,
and the Passion of Jesus on bronze
Stations of the Cross.

The empty church doesn't inspire awe
as High Mass often did
with organ tones, choir singing,
vases of roses on altars,
priests in elaborate vestments
and incense in the air.

As we walk towards the main altar,
I remember a time when a priest uttered,
"You son-of-a-bitch—"
when an altar boy tripped
on his over-sized surplice,
fell, and smashed the Bible onto the floor.

We two other altar boys gathered the cover,
sections of the book,
loose pages and carried them to Father Luke.
He assembled the pages in blessed silence.

After that, I served Father Luke

water and wine, and he ordered me
to return to the side altar for more wine,
for he insisted I fill the chalice to the brim.

We kneel at a front pew, and Gail prays
that our team will win the homecoming
football game.

Praying seems unfair.
I don't say anything to Gail.
I was taught to share my heresies
in the confessional with a priest.

MY SISTER VERONICA

I stop at your grave,
a granite stone just level
with the cut grass,
place an orange rose
in the flower vase.

Remember picnics at Cheyenne River
with our vast and curious clan?
Some of our uncles wore bib-overalls,
denim shirts and straw hats. They stuck
bamboo fishing poles into the riverbank,
watched red and white bobbers for nibbles or strikes.
Our mom and aunts commandeered ice chests,
picnic baskets, and blankets, while gossiping
about absent relatives and their ailments.
They nibbled on sunflower seeds and sipped iced tea.

We cousins plunged into the murky water,
doing cannonballs and belly flops.
Swimming and diving below the surface,
we bumped into bullheads and perch.
Devouring hotdogs, potato salad and Kool-Aid
under the clear skies and bright sun,
we lounged on sweet prairie grass,
breathed in air filled with scents of cut hay
and maturing clover crops,
listened to twittering meadowlarks.

Afternoons we played tag, softball, and flew kites,
until we dropped back into the water to cool off.
If our dad and uncles caught enough fish,
we lingered into evening, with mosquitoes and wasps,

ate fried fish potatoes, with fresh vegetables,
and sucked down more Kool-Aid.
Remember the rides home in our old Chevy—
two parents with six kids on top of each other
like calves in a trailer on the way to market?

Dear sweet, Veronica,
born June 1, 1937,
died June 1, 1937,
you don't remember any of it.

HITCHHIKING

The only time I ever hitchhiked,
my thumb attracted the driver
of a sixteen wheeler.
He said he needed
company to stay awake,
been on the road for eighteen hours,
hauling a huge caterpillar
on the back of his rig.

I was headed to my home town
a hundred miles away
to visit friends,
cruise familiar streets,
and dance to rock and roll.

Nodding his head
for me to climb in,
he reached for second gear,
then slumped forward
onto the steering wheel.

Panicked he might be dead,
I shouted and shook
his shoulder fiercely.

In one smooth move, he woke,
stopped the truck and asked,
Do you know how to drive?
I said I'd driven grain trucks on farms.
We exchanged places, and he told me
to double clutch between forward gears.
Then he fell asleep.

When I reached forty miles per hour,
the road looked narrow like a path on the prairies,
and the speed seemed like sixty.

The first town I entered, and the only one
I would pass through with a stoplight,
I tried to slow,
but I didn't think to double clutch
down through the gears.
Thank goodness it was dinnertime
and few drivers were on the main street.

The next stop was my hometown.
I managed to halt the truck on the outskirts.
The driver awakened and thanked me.
I was still shaking as I climbed out of the truck
and stepped down onto the safety of solid ground.

BURIAL GROUND (1963)

Bright sun reflects off the icy snow pack near the
shores of Lake Sacajawea. I walk on what was once
Hidatsa land before a dam flooded the people to higher
ground. Long before the deluge, Mandan Indians, a
tribe decimated by smallpox-infected blankets, joined
the Hidatsa. Four Bears, a Mandan Chief, who had once
welcomed all travelers, said after many deaths that white
men were "Black Hearted Dogs."

Carrying a rifle to give a reason for this hike, I amble
across the headlands of the lake, cross ravines, stay
above the thick brush. The silence seems odd—just the
crunching of my steps—given the past of these prairies
when buffalo pounded the ground like an earthquake,
and where wolves howled in unison for no reason at all
but to make claim to these vast open spaces. Delighting
in the visible reaches of the terrain and exalting in the
lengthy strides of seasoned legs, I ramble on, lucky to be
alone.

As the afternoon dims, gray clouds build up in the
northwest, driven by a slight breeze. Knowing how zero
degree, sunny weather can deteriorate into a fierce storm
in as little as an hour, I start back to my car a mile away.
Retracing my steps across the tops of ravines, I feel the
wind come up, driving snow at an angle out of rolling
charcoal clouds. I pull the hood of my parka over my
stocking cap and trudge sideways to keep frostbite at
bay.

Halfway to my car I stop again over a ravine that is dark
and deep. I listen to the whisper of the wind passing

through the brush below. Captivated by its haunting quality, I take a few steps down. The sound becomes eerie, a wailing in high notes. I draw back, recall a map that marked the burial grounds of the Hidatsa. I am near those submerged sites, just fifty feet below the water's icy surface. I imagine the collapsed scaffolds that had supported the dead high above the ground, resting now on the lake bottom with an occasional catfish or pike nipping at the buffalo hide fastenings. Frightened as much by the sounds in the air and images in my mind as by the growing fury of the storm, I rush towards safety. My only guides are my nearly filled footprints. The snow is falling in large flakes against the black clouds that skim the hillside.

DEPARTURE

I

I couldn't find you in the faces of older men,
in books, movies, or even dreams.
It was no use. I had to invent you
since your residue was everywhere.

Arriving on a late night flight,
I found you waiting at baggage claim.
You drove because you knew a shortcut
through residential streets, but stopped
half a block away from a traffic light—
Were your eyes that bad?
You, who once hurled a daredevil
eighty feet to sink where pickerel hid,
or brought down a pheasant on the wing
at sixty yards, not for sport or pleasure,
but food. The next day when I drove
you told me where to park at Miracle Mart—
To avoid a search for your pickup truck later?

At your favorite watering hole,
you drank boilermakers
and asked about children and grandchildren.
After each sequence of questions you sang a tune,
If you don't do it when you first have a chance,
you won't get to do it at all.
You won't get to do it at all.

II

Another time and place,
you raged against life,
including me, in the foulest language.
Howling and weaving about,
your eyes flashed red.
The flesh on your forehead
protruded into two horn-like bumps.
Your mouth ceased moving,
and smoke steamed from your nose.
I stared into your eyes
until you whimpered and collapsed
into a lawn chair.
Your forehead felt clammy, cool to my hand.
"Damn it, don't touch me."

III

A nurse's call pulled me from sleep.
You had slipped out of your lounge chair to the floor.
You didn't call out for help
but just lay there.
When she entered, you said,
"I suppose I should get up."

"No real harm, just bruises,"
she told me from that distant time zone.

"He's survived many falls to the floor."

IV

Burn, rave, and rage
shadowed you at every turn.
These words, written for another, suited you,
so I read Dylan Thomas at your bedside
among the mourners.

You, however, didn't wait,
didn't storm and bellow,
but chose to just slip off,
leaving me to recall your measures:
    A serious drinker, flushing your dentures down the toilet,
    A non-voter, holding forth like a political zealot,
    A newspaper skimmer, telling wry stories,
    An old man, sallying forth to bump and grind.
I laughed and laughed—
the response you preferred—
until tears scalded my face.

IMMIGRANT

Just off the Dakota Badlands
on one-time Sioux treaty land,
my great-grandfather Martin
stalked through sweet grass
on his hilly, rocky farm,
a shotgun cradled in his arms.
He searched for wild turkeys,
stone figures hiding
in the brush line of a coulee.
His youngest son followed behind,
carrying two grouse by their necks,
victims of his papa's deadly aim.

Martin's face wore disappointment,
not just because two grouse
weren't enough for his large family's table,
but because the forces of history
carved a life that weeping
could not touch anymore.

Uprooted twice, he left three brothers
and one sister behind in South Russia.
One brother was shot in the face
by Bolsheviks trying to extort tribute.
The remaining siblings died
of hunger, heartbreak, and violence
during Stalin's rule and World War II.

After he lost his wife in childbirth
with their tenth child to a Texas grave,
Martin chose to homestead
in North Dakota on barren land.

DEPARTURE IN 1893

I

Thorbjorg turns to look back
at her fishing village—
birth place and home for seventeen years.
Small wood frame houses near the water
huddle together like a flock of seabirds
in cold, gray mists.
A few bluewater fishing boats sway,
anchored in the fjord.
Rowboats rest upon the shore.
A famine has descended on the island,
like winter storms at sea
during fishing season,
taking many lives.

Her parents, Thorvald and Lara,
will live in this village
until they rest above on a shelf of land
known as the Holy Ground.

Thorbjorg will not miss her father's
drinking bouts after arctic fishing voyages.
She will not miss filleting cod,
hanging them on high racks to dry,
or butchering whales on the beach.
She will not miss the dark, rainy weather,
or the treeless, volcanic soil.

II

Thorbjorg follows the wagon trail on foot,
hauling on her shoulder, a bag
stuffed with clothes, healing herbs,
dried codfish, a Bible,
a few kronur, and passage papers
for a ship sailing to Canada.

As she plods along at a funeral's pace,
a ptarmigan, with mottled blackish body,
wings, tail and red eye combs,
flies from the boggy meadow
of cotton grass, buttercups and dandelions.
She pauses to wonder if she will see this bird,
again, or hear the cooing of a golden plover,
or the warbling trill of a whimbrel
in her adopted land ahead.

III

Her ship will sail out of Akureyri in six days.
She must pick up her pace, for it will take
four days or more to walk to that port city.
When she climbs out of the fjord
past rugged, rock walls,
the caves remind her of the *Hidden People*
who are known to help travelers.

Thorbjorg rests in empty churches,
reads Psalms and snacks on dried fish.
Evenings, she stops at crofts,

small farms in Iceland,
for bed and board.

She continues her journey across
the ocean to Canada to
an Icelandic community of Saskatchewan,
where she knows it is her duty
to create new life.

THE HOLY GROUND

On this day without end,
in this land of volcanoes and hot springs,
in this place of poets and legends,
over the graves of my earliest
known maternal forebears,
I am bundled in down
just below the Arctic Circle,
standing on a basalt plateau.

Two sets of four white stone posts
mark a shelf of land above Saudarkrokur, Iceland.

Great-grandfather Thorvaldur, born in 1851,
at sea from age fourteen in open boats,
pounded ice from gunnels and bailed sea water,
while towing whales to split upon the beach below.
Chilled from the frigid sea,
he drank deeply of aquavit.
Thorvaldur died at 70 on the first day of 1921.

Great-grandmother Lara, born in 1843,
mother of Petur and Hildur Margaret,
arrived at Saudarkrokur from Iceland's eastern shore.
A healer, she practiced midwifery and herbalism.
Skilled in handicraft,
she fashioned out of heather,
wreaths and crucifixes for graves.
Lara died at 77 in 1920.

As wife of Thorvaldur, Lara gave birth to four.
Twins died in infancy.
Thorbjorg and Gudron Olof survived.

Thorbjorg, my grandmother, born in 1876,
became known to us as Bertha.

Bertha is buried far from her parents,
in the land of prairies and farms
where wind blows south from Canada.

TIMES PAST

When winter winds begin to blow,
and madrone trees twist and crack,
my thoughts turn to times long ago.

To work, family, and foe,
to failure to accept with tact,
when winter winds begin to blow.

Memory fades and faces flow
in shadows haunting fact.
My thoughts turn to times long ago.

When triumphs were few and done for show,
diminishing to inaction.
When winter winds begin to blow.

My body growls and joints glow.
Sudden pains take my breath aback.
My thoughts turn to times long ago.

Spirit resists failure to know,
urges the body to action.
When winter winds begin to blow,
my thoughts turn to times long ago.

II ENCOUNTERS

DESERT

A solitary tarantula
scurries off the trail
to security behind a large stone.

Saguaro cacti guard the arroyo,
balance precariously on steep slopes.

Coyote cubs scramble from a den,
yelp at mother's return.

A burro brays, asserts his claim
against intruders.

At the summit of Big Horn peak, I survey
this city of two million people
that arose on the ruins of the Hohokam.
Many of the newcomers are retirees,
fearing the rivers will dry
and the aquifers will empty.

Later, driving north
over Granite pass,
I descend the winding road
to the Colorado River.

Across the bridge,
an oasis of casinos lines the bank,
with acres of parking lot
filled with buses and cars.

I join the congregation
at the casino, where worshippers

address themselves to the rush
of tumblers and silver.

These modern services sting
like mistletoe on a paloverde tree.

DANGERS ON THE SLOPES

I

We quit removing our crampons
when someone yells, "Listen!"
We hear *skip, skip, skip,*
and see up at the top of the slope
a boulder bounding down
toward us.

One of our leaders, alone
in the center of the chute,
judges the rock's angle of flight,
leaps and leans his body away.

The stone plunges by
just missing his head.

I hear a few "lucks with us"
and one "lucky guy!"

We're all shaken,
but we glissade down the slope,
ice axes as rudders.

I call to my rope partner,
"We're lucky it wasn't an avalanche."

II

The last team to cross Nisqually Glacier
above a huge crevasse,
my partner shouts "Falling!"

I dive onto the slope,
plunge my ice axe and
crampon-fitted boots into the ice.

His weight drags me
a foot, ripping ice,
sending snow into my face.
I'm sweating, blinded,
fearing I won't see my wife
and two young children again.

After what seems like an hour,
I spy my partner laying spread eagle
just feet from the gaping crevasse.

He shouts he's okay and has his ice axe.
I belay him as he steps up the slope.

We continue, carefully
using kick steps,
until we reach the safety
of base camp,
my last on any mountain.

ENCOUNTERS IN CHINA

I

A rickshaw convoy sweeps through
the narrow streets of a hutong,
past steps and beside walls
of the homes of long–ago
advisors to Emperors.

Inside the enclosures,
one-story flats open onto courtyards,
now sheltering extended families.

One tall, amused rickshaw driver
poses for a photographer,
smiles, and raises an index finger,
apropos of what?

II

On a market street in Chongqing
where laundry hangs from the windows
of heavily-sooted brick apartments,
a man proudly poses
with his year-old son for visitors.

A vendor on the sidewalk
stir-fries meat and vegetables in a wok,
on his makeshift stove
poised on an upturned barrel.

People gamble and play mahjong
under a tent at a wake.

In back of them is a coffin.
The dead man's photo hangs above it.

These mourners stare past our group,
seem to see through us
as if we are spirits.

III

In a factory in Shanghai
three young women
sit side-by-side at a loom,
weaving a silk rug.

Hour upon hour, and day after day,
for two years they pass a bobbin
and comb down silk thread
into intricate pattern and color.

Not knowing that the farms
these weavers came from
are under water from the backwaters
of the Three Gorges Dam,
we buy the beauty these women create
at bargain prices.

MARTIN'S HIKES

Plodding up First Hill,
Martin takes short steps.

He enters the medical building,
registers and sits in the reception
room where some women wear wigs.
A few elderly patients use walkers.
Some have partners to encourage.
Others have only bandages
around the inside crook of their elbows.

Martin's name is called.
He enters the room,
stretches out on a table,
legs secured in molded plastic forms
under an IMRT exterior beam
radiation machine with
Calypso guidance system.

The IMRT circles his body,
stopping beneath,
above, and to each side,
swinging into place,
bobbing as it goes
with short bursts of beam
to target his prostate.

Martin is midway
in his nine-week treatment.
He reflects on the consequences
of the cure he chose for his affliction.
Will he lose bladder control,
become constipated,

impotent,
metastatic?
Will he regret his decision?

Nevertheless, he jests with friends
about secret meetings
with Ms. Calypso
who daily hovers above
his pelvic bones.

RED WINE GLASS

Tom attempted a doctoral dissertation
on Thomas De Quincey
but lacked the moxie to finish it.
His only bride-to-be
dropped him for another.

He passed his time as a professor
of English and with weekend work
on his boat, adding a deck,
a cabin, and a cockpit with steering wheel.
More time passed building
and then installing two masts,
an engine, and cabin controls.

Tom towed his sailboat hull
down Port Washington Narrows
to a boat construction building.
He labored there to finish his
thirty-two-foot double-ended ketch.

On sabbatical leave from his professorial post,
Tom returned to his place of youth
where he first mastered sailing.
He celebrated his fifty-fifth birthday there
by placing an order for red sails,
and that same night he died of a heart attack
without ever sailing into blue waters.

TERRITORIAL NEMESIS

I

Our blue point Siamese Salt
spots a cocker spaniel in our driveway
and leaps off the railing,
over the lawn, claws first
into the dog's back.

Barking and bucking like a bronco,
the dog rushes off our property.

II

Our neighbor knocks on our door
to ask if we'd like to buy her car.
Salt had chased her male cat
through an open window
where they fought,
shredding the car's seats
and scenting the vehicle
with odorous yearn.

III

Another came to our house to tell us
he caught our blue point in his house,
eating out of his cat's food bowl.

"Where's my cat now? I asked.

He walked to his car, opened the trunk
and pointed to a cardboard box.
"Don't open it. That cat's wild."

I undid the lid, lifted out Salt,
and he purred in my arms.

TORTOISESHELL

When I give more than gentle pets
to my tortoiseshell Matilda,
pull her ears or rub her neck,
she rolls over, hisses, bares her claws,
leaps to the floor, and runs out the door.

In our garden, among rows of carrots,
marigolds and raspberry bushes,
Matilda stalks
in a belly-dragging crouch,
like a savanna lioness,
tail swaying, brushing the soil.

Matilda springs in a blur.
Doves scatter away,
and squirrels chatter up the trees.
Sparrows, moles, and garter snakes
aren't as fortunate.

HORSE CHESTNUT

A century after your sapling
ocean voyage from London's Kew Gardens
to a park on Bainbridge Island,
your cape of thick foliage
slopes down wide shoulders
to just above your ankles
like Rodin's statue of Balzac.

As a boy, I culled chestnuts,
carried them home to soak in varnish.
Once dry, I attached them to strings
to use as weapons in conker's games.

Long, pear-shaped leaves
hang from thin green stems.
Pink blossoms stand like candelabras
straight up above the clusters of leaves,
nurturing hummingbirds and honeybees.
Pieces of blossom float to the ground,
carpeting fallen chestnuts,
orchard grass, fern leaf yarrow.
Squirrels scamper to bury food.

Rivalries of birds,
coyotes after prey,
drought, blight, fierce icy winds,
heavy snow on your limbs,
threats of gnawing chainsaws
from the encroaching
condos and commerce
have assaulted your presence.

Yet here you stand,
trunk solid
through passing years,
adding ring after ring
to your girth.

MADRONE

For Madeline DeFrees

Dry leaves rust from your iron boughs
descend along your leathery skin,
your crown a circular repose.

Your fifty feet in self-mulched ground,
feeding from fluids in veins so thin,
dry leaves rust from your iron boughs.

As growth rings tell of many seasons found,
pink blossoms promise more to win,
your crown a circular repose.

When woodpeckers tap scored bark to the ground,
pile mulch to your shin,
dry leaves rust from your iron boughs.

If white pigeons fall upon your red rounds,
hallucinate along your limbs,
your crown a circular repose.

Madrone, evergreen tree of Puget Sound,
you live on and thrive with all your kin.
Dry leaves rust from your iron boughs.
Your crown a circular repose.

III AFFINITIES

NATURAL AFFINITIES

Like a sudden, late spring storm
that drives golf ball-sized hail,
leaving divots on a fairway,
a dark mood settles in unannounced.

Maybe writer's block, a poor score
on the links, or a quarrel with one's spouse
fosters the feeling that hangs on
and churns the mind.

But like the abrupt storm that succumbs
to a balmy round of fresh air and sunshine,
the mood swings and the imagination awakens
to balmy dreams and maybe even a poem.

DOUBLE VISION

For Mary Lou Sanelli

I practice a ritual before going to bed—
I look out my bedroom window
to an apartment across the way
to see if a light is shining.
A poet does night work there.

She writes about neighbors,
chance meetings with friends,
exchanging flowers for tomatoes,
meeting at a pub for drinks,
and leaving notes
under windshield wipers and doors.

One night I peek from a different room
and am startled to find
I've been seeing it wrong—
a streetlight reflects off the poet's window.

Now I only take my look
from the bedroom window
where I know for certain
the poet's flame continues to burn.

DENISE LEVERTOV

A transplant first from England,
then from the East Coast
to Seattle's Seward Park area,
Denise lived near heron
in view of Mt. Rainier.

I met her first by phone.
She drove a hard bargain
to give a keynote address
at our writers' conference.

She was worth it,
not just for her words and presence,
but also for our long conversation
about our family histories.

A moment of high glee came when
I told her I was a "retired" Catholic,
a faith she had just joined.

Her funeral wasn't
the last time I saw Denise.
In Seward Park, seated on a bench
to eat an apple, I gazed at lily pads
and other dense foliage
and caught sight of a heron
sitting on a post in the water.

The bird squawked,
then hopped to another post
directly in front of me.

I immediately thought it was she
and drifted into memories
of our long conversation.

When I looked up again,
the heron was gone.
I had missed its flight.

IN MEMORY OF WILLIAM STAFFORD

Oregonians feel the earth shudder.

Ducks stray from their flight path.

Salmon pause in their upstream struggle.

Wolves sniff the breeze,
searching for the scent of trouble.

Former students gather to mourn
their friend and professor.

Poets lower their standards,
read their poems out loud.

KEY WEST, FLORIDA
January 1993

I

In the morning before dawn
full moon shines on Duval Street
like a stage work light.

The only sounds:
a cat's cry,
a rooster's crow.

Two men, dreaming in Spanish,
sleep, uncovered, on a street level porch.

Balconies hang over storefronts
that shelter bikinis and Havana hats.

A woman of the night makes a last call
at a pay phone.
A sign above her head reads:
Catfish and hushpuppies, thirteen-fifty.

Wahoo and Amberjack decorate
the back wall of Uncle Louie's diner.
Soon he'll serve real Cuban coffee
at the Formica counter.

Later, locals will eat conch fritters
and callaloo in cafes
that welcome poets.

II

A half-century ago
you strolled down Duval Street
under palm and mangrove trees,
floating on the scent of jasmine.

After dining on green turtle consommé,
oysters, rice, and mangoes,
you did rumba night at Sloppy Joe's.

You reveled in folk art, wood carvings
and paper flowers,
pitied the convicts,
at large during the day
locked-out at night,
and told stories of fortunetellers.

Elizabeth Bishop, in exile,
composed poems, penned letters,
and practiced "One Art."

SANCTUARY

I wander the world unfettered
by such trivialities
as money and transportation.

Snowflakes float down
under a street lamp.

I plow through drifts
and spring up steps
to wide, double library doors.

Inside, warm air carries
the fragrance of books
and carnauba wax.

My parka draped over a chair,
I stand with my back to a radiator,
letting heat drive out the chill.

Once inside the stacks of books,
I thumb through photographs,
and visit the Sahara Desert.

Perhaps next I'll climb aboard the *Pequot*
or visit with my friends Tom and Huck.

ANDALUSIA

While in Andalusia,
stop at Granada and visit the Alhambra—
its gardens and pools triggered
Washington Irving's imagination.

Stroll through Lorca's Memorial Garden,
a tribute to dance,
deep song and bullfighting.

Row upon row
of flowering shrubs circle his home,
remind you to lay bouquets
in the Granada hills
where Franco's Army buried him.

Climb to the Albaicin quarter,
near some gypsy caves,
and lunch on media barca.

Enter a luthier's shop below on a hillside street
to view beautiful acoustic guitars.
Be patient and stay,
even if you must decline the offer
to try out one of these
rosewood and spruce sculptures,
for at any moment a guitarist will walk in
and pull one off the wall.

He will likely begin by running through scales,
chords, and arpeggios,
listening intently for just the right tone
and maybe a false string vibration.

When he begins to play,
say a tune by Albeniz, maybe "Zambra Granadina,"
a woman, whom you hadn't seen,
raises her arms and claps a set of castanets.

Slowly, she swivels her body and clicks her heels
in rhythmic counterpoint to
the visceral bass notes of the guitar
and the luthier's staccato clapping
and high-pitched singing.

Before long the three will take you
to that place
of mystery and spirit,
a place called duende.

CUBAN COFFEE

Pouring hot water
over freshly ground
coffee beans and chicory,
the arched stream flows
until the mixture floats
to the top of the filter,
misting a fragrant steam.

I inhale the aroma and imagine Cuba:
coral reefs, cays, beaches,
brown-skinned bodies in bikinis,
sweet scents of hand-rolled cigars,
sugar plantations,
marshes,
Sierra Maestra peaks.

The dark liquid trickles
slow as maple syrup.

Bubbles form in a froth
like soap balloons,
shiny and bluish.

Grounds cling to
the sides of the filter,
offer my fortune for the day.

Pouring more water,
I drive the remaining grounds down,
enriching the flavor

of the coffee below,
while erasing a map
of what fate
had in store for me.

LAKE QUINAULT RAIN FOREST

(Aftermath of three days of sustained 125 mph
winds in December of 2007)

The root ball of a toppled old growth cedar
rose fifteen feet high and wide,
carving a deep hole in the trail.

A second ancient cedar had landed
across another, splitting its trunk with
innards exposed and sap dry
as a deer carcass at a roadside.

I twisted my way through
downed cedars,
plus a few fir, spruce,
and the trunk of a pine tree
that had been severed
of its thirty foot top
about ten feet above the ground.
Sap had dripped down its face,
forming a two-foot high waterfall.

My ankles and knees ached at the joints,
calf and thigh muscles are sore,
reminded me of a distant, future falling.

A LUCKY CRAB

I reach my destination on Hood Canal
before the rush of high tide.

My fifteen-foot boat drifts out
to a depth of ninety feet
at the edge of a drop-off below.

I lower a pot until it disappears
below dark, dense algae
and settles on the seafloor.

Every fifty yards, I drop other pots,
until a line of white and red buoys
dance over low waves like
fishing bobbers.

I imagine the odor
of salmon heads luring large,
male crabs up slopes
from the depths.

After an hour of fly fishing,
I power back to my first buoy,
to raise the pot.

Teeming with Dungeness crab,
claws rattle and struggle
against each other.
One crab continues to feed on fish,
another reaches for my fingers.

I toss the large males into a bucket,

all except for the one that
rips into the salmon head.
He has a miniature claw
and a dogged determination.

Although legal, I flip him
back into the water.

SCHOONER

A sailboat rests at moorage,
roped to a dock across Eagle Harbor.
The rays of the early morning sun
glisten off its white hull.

I sit at breakfast table,
greet the Ragland
by tipping my coffee cup.

As if in response,
there's a slight movement
of its masts and lines.

The schooner's motion suggests
it's tired of sleep,
wants to fill its sails,
swing into the wind,
take a heading for the open sea.

I'm happy to see this blue water vessel,
a touchstone that tells me
I'm still alive,
at rest,
but longing for the next voyage
to distant places
or just a stroll down the road.

ABOUT THE AUTHOR

David Hecker's literary life started when two teachers
introduced him to the correct usage of English, to authors,
books, libraries, and a desire to teach others. He earned a
BA in English at Minot State Teachers College, an MA in
English Education at the University of Minnesota, and a
Ph.D. in American Studies at Washington State University.
He lectured students at Olympic College in English and
American culture. Up to this time he wrote prose works
for academic conferences, book reviews, travel logs, and
articles for local newspapers and historical journals.

David also received three NEH Grants for research and
for program development. His writing shifted to literary
genres after he co-founded the Olympic College Writers'
Conference, directed it for five years and edited annually
a conference chapbook titled *Signals*. Meeting with and
scheduling writers like William Stafford, Madeline De
Frees, Denise Levertov and Marvin Bell for keynote
addresses at the conferences were in part causes for the
shift in his writing. During the writers' conference period

he also explored creative writing in fiction and poetry at the University of Washington's evening extension program, at Port Townsend's annual Centrum Writers' Conference and with various local writers' groups.

He received an award from NLAPW, Seattle Branch, for his poem "Earth Map", an award from the Washington Poets Association for his poem "Acoma Pueblo," and publication in a series of journals including *Exhibition, Paper Boat, Poets West, Ars Poetica* and *Cirque Journal*. He also published *Full Circle: A Journey in Search of Roots,* a memoir in 2012; *Strangers Before the Bench,* a historical novel in 2014. Letterpress publication of poetry broadsides and pamphlets have been done, and hopefully poetry chapbooks with wood block illustrations are scheduled for the future.

David lives on Bainbridge Island with wife, Helen, and visits frequently with family members in the vicinity.

CPSIA information can be obtained
at www.ICGtesting.com
Printed in the USA
FFOW05n0550100217

9 781936 657254